What Is The Difference Between A Wife Material Woman & A Non-Wife Material Woman?

By: Aaron Fields

ISBN: 978-1-953962-362

Table Of Contents:

<u>Something To Think About Before You Read</u>

Women are beautiful human beings, but not all of them are wife material. ------------
Aaron Fields

Word From The Author

Gentlemen, it's very important that you know what you want out of life, especially as it pertains to the relationships you form with women. Can a man have one woman? Yes, he can. Can a man have more than one woman? Yes, he can, even though western society may disagree. Whatever it is you decide to do as a man, make sure you are fully aware and meticulous in your decision making when dealing with women.

Did I just say a man can have multiple women? Yes, I said that, just in case you were wondering. However, it's important for the man to understand that the number of women you bring into your life can be associated with the amount of stress and negative energy you may have to put up with. If you're a man that deals with women, especially on an intimate level, you must make sure that your life is in order first. Are you financially stable? Is being physically and mentally stable a priority in your life? Are you spiritually healthy? These are the important questions you must ask yourself before you bring a woman into your life.

Why does a man have to be healthy and stable in every aspect of his life before he gets with a woman? Well, it's because when a woman comes into your life, she's going to demand a lot of your time, money, attention, and energy. Your partner can either bring chaos, confusion, and destruction into your life or help you stay focused and on the right path.

If you're not content with your current life situation, it might be best to avoid serious relationships with women for now. Although this is just my perspective, I urge you guys to consider this as a viable option. Why? Well, because it's important that you guys understand the value of investing in yourself before bringing other people into your life. Saying yes to a woman who is interested in you isn't always the right choice, especially if you're not where you want to be in life.

If you're a man who enjoys being with multiple women, make sure you're honest and upfront with all of them. There is no need to lie and create this false narrative that you're a "one woman man". That's only going to aggravate the situation and make matters worse. As a man, it's important that you are being straightforward with the things you want out of life. If you want to pursue multiple women, it's best to be honest about it. Believe it or not, a lot of women in this society are fine with certain men having relationships with multiple women. Most women love it when a man is desired by multiple women because it generates competition, excitement, and drama.

However, you decide to deal with women, make sure you don't develop an unhealthy obsession. Keep in mind women are beautiful and valuable people, but there's no need to be obsessed with them. A man's decision in a wife is one of the most significant choices he'll make in his life, aside from his profession success. A major way you can tell if a woman is a wife, or a non-wife material woman will be based on how she conducts herself and how you're compelled to interact with her. It's important for you guys to understand that based on how a woman dresses, acts, and conducts herself is going to say a lot about her as a person. In this book, you will learn the distinct qualities of a wife material woman and a non-wife material woman.

Chapter 1

A Man's First Love

A man's first love should be his gifts and his vision in life. Every man on earth dominates a certain area of his life with his gifts, which is why his gift and vision should be his first love and top priority. When a man finds his gift, he discovers a vision for his life. The man who discovers his identity and talent lives a meaningful life.

On this earth, whatever happens to humanity depends on what happens to the man. That's why it's important for men to be protectors, providers, leaders, and teachers. The goal for the man is to discover himself and become the best version of himself through self-manifestation.

Before you find a woman, make sure you know your vision and your purpose in life. Sometimes you'll come across a few women in your life that will try to compete with your dreams and aspirations because they want to be the top priority. The reason behind the anger and confusion of most women in this society is because of the lack of self-awareness and personal growth among men.

What are your gifts? Are you good at something? What is your vision? Are you at peace? Are you fulfilled? Have you discovered yourself yet? It's always important for a man to realize that he is not here on this earth for an experiment; he's here for an assignment.

Chapter 2

Don't Let Her Interrupt Your Flow

Is there something you're you passionate about? What skills are you blessed with? What is it that keeps you motivated? Whatever it is, it's important that you become proficient at it. Why? Well, because sometimes certain people will come into your life to see if they can interrupt your flow.

When a man is motivated and focused on pursuing his dreams, a woman might attempt to interrupt his flow. Some women do this intentionally to bring chaos and confusion into the man's life. Sometimes women want to see if they can divert the man by leading him away from his life's mission.

Keep in mind a non-wife material woman will go to great lengths to bring destruction and hardship into a man's life. Unlike the non-wife, a wife material woman is someone who will go to great lengths to fit into the man's life by making things better for him. It's important for men to understand that if a woman is not concerned with your health, well-being and peace of mind, leave the situation and move on with your life.

With the world already being hard and stressful, why would a man want to make things even harder by inviting a toxic woman into his life? Although not all women, most of them seem to be attracted to chaos and dysfunction in this society. It's vital for men to set the rules of engagement with women they interact with. It's important to communicate to the woman/women that there are certain things you won't put up with. Based on the energy the women are going to bring into your life, it's your job to figure out if they're worth dealing with. Unfortunately, many of you guys allow some of these women to overstep their boundaries. Why? Because you find them physically attractive. Just because a woman is beautiful, that doesn't mean she gets to bring negativity into your life.

Chapter 3

A Non-Wife Material Woman Doesn't Respect Order

A man with wisdom and intelligence will seek peace, structure, and order. Most non-wife material women in this society don't respect order because they prefer chaos and confusion. Women who are not wife material think that their looks can make up for their dysfunctional behavior in a relationship.

Whatever you want to pursue in life as a man, just know that the non-wife material woman wants you to put her first above your aspirations. Believe it or not, most women get an exciting thrill when they're able to come into a man's life and become his number one priority. Although it's important to treat women with love and respect, they should not be glorified or treated like a deity.

When a non-wife material woman sees that you're motivated and focused, she will try to distract you and convince you to put more of your attention on her. If a woman is trying to get you to worship her, that's a major red flag. Why do most non-wife material women want men to become overly infatuated with them? It's because they want to control and manipulate men into doing things that serve the interests of women

If a non-wife material woman makes a man worship her, she will probably become bored and reveal more of her negative traits. To put it differently, she will show her true colors. Therefore, it's important for men to vet and evaluate the women they bring into their lives. Just because she likes you at first doesn't guarantee those feelings will endure.

Chapter 4

A Wife Material Woman Respects Order

Now what does a wife material woman look like? For starters, a wife material woman exhibits discipline, virtue, and good manners. A wife material woman who is genuine will not intentionally bring destruction into your life.

Unlike the non-wife material woman, the wife material woman will not interrupt your flow. In fact, the wife material woman will make sure that she does not bring any negativity or instability into the man's life. Why? It's because a wife material woman respects order. Not only does a wife material woman respects masculine characteristics, but she also embraces her true essence.

Why does a wife material woman respect order? It's because she knows that having a strong, astute, and spiritually strong man in her life can bring her more stability and peace. Now, in most cases, non-wife material women don't respect order because they embrace toxicity.

Be alert if a woman is attempting to coerce your thoughts or feelings about her. Why? Well, because if you have strong feelings for someone, it will develop naturally. Women who try to control your emotions display dysfunctional behavior. The presence of a woman in your life should be a source of joy, not stress. Remember, it's your responsibility as a man to contribute to her happiness as well. To achieve this, you need to bring stability, positivity, and inspiration into her life.

Food For Thought:

Although I'm saying a lot of things about women right now, it's imperative that men understand how important it is to make your woman's life better. If you're in a woman's life and you're trying to see how much damage you can create for her, leave her alone, re-evaluate yourself and get your life together. A man is not supposed to bring any negativity or instability into the woman's life.

What are some positive things you can bring into a woman's life?

_____

_____

_____

_____

_____

What are some positive things a woman needs to bring into your life?

_____

_____

_____

_____

_____

_____

_____

Advice

Although it's important to focus on your aspirations, it's also important that you don't become obsessed with your goals. Our craft can become an object of worship if we work on it excessively. The goal is to always maintain a healthy balance and keep things in moderation. From a biblical standpoint, never put earthly things on a pedestal, only spiritual things.

Thoughts:

_____

_____

_____

_____

_____

_____

Chapter 5

Non-Wife Material Women Are Disrespectful

If a woman is always conducting herself inappropriately, she's most likely a non-wife material woman. A woman who doesn't respect manhood, masculinity, or authority is likely a low-quality woman. As a man, it's very important that the woman you're with respects you.

Why do non-wife material women say disrespectful things to the men that they're with? Well, there are many layers and answers to this question. However, most of the time, women will say disrespectful things to men because they want to emasculate him. Many men continue to experience this because they lack self-respect. When a man doesn't hold himself in high regard, he shouldn't expect others to treat him with respect.

The reason non-wife material women like to make inflammatory statements towards men is because they are testing you. They want to see if they can provoke an emotional reaction from the man. Or maybe they want to see if the man will fall for their chicanery.

As a man, once you're able to understand the nature of the woman, you should know how to operate when you're around them. A man should never allow himself to get confused and frustrated over a woman. Don't allow the woman's rhetoric or manipulation tactics to cause you to lose sight of who you are. Either the woman is bringing pleasure, peace and comfort into your life or she's not. If the low-quality woman is not worthy of being taken seriously, make sure you don't get her pregnant. If you're an astute and upstanding man and the low-quality woman knows that you don't take her seriously, she's going to see what she can take from you. Therefore, you should be very careful and keep a watchful eye.

Chapter 6

Is She Jealous of Your Aspirations?

One of the many things that non-wife material women hate the most is being second place on a man's priority list. When a man puts his aspirations before the woman, she may get jealous. As a man, if you're not careful, a desperate woman will try to sabotage your goals.

Gentlemen, if you have major goals you want to accomplish in your life, it may be best for you to embrace solitude for a while. If a man is on a path to achieving something great, it may not be in his best interest to be in a serious relationship with a woman right now. However, if you decide to get with a woman, make sure it's the type of woman that's going to bring peace, comfort, and support into your life.

Always remember that toxic women will continue to bring negativity into your life if you allow them to. Having a toxic person in your life will prevent you from achieving your goals. It's important to understand that sometimes in life, you have to be by yourself in order to reach your goals. In case you don't know this already, hanging out with toxic people will get you nowhere in life.

Be sure to associate with individuals who are motivated, disciplined, and committed to improving their way of life. Why? Well, because you don't want to surround yourself with envious people. Toxic, insecure, and envious people will go to any lengths to bring down those who are doing well for themselves.

As it pertains to women, it's going to be up to you as the man to decide on the type of women you want to deal with. Based on how the woman conducts herself is going to determine how you're going to deal with her. For example, if a woman is loyal, faithful, and respectful towards you, then that means she goes higher on the totem pole. When the woman is being disrespectful and not conducting herself appropriately, it's time to stop engaging with her. The overall point I'm trying to make to you guys is that men must be honest with themselves about the type of women they choose to deal with. No matter how the woman conducts herself, always remember that you cannot control her. The only person you can control is yourself.

Chapter 7

Not Every Woman Cares About You

Although life can be complex sometimes, life is also simple, depending on how you view your circumstances. Paying attention to your surroundings is key to identifying the people that care about you. Believe it or not, there are very few people in this world that are concerned with your happiness and well-being.

Hopefully, if you find someone who loves, respects, and appreciates you, make sure you give that same positive energy back to them. For some strange reason, many men today assume that all the women they sleep around with care about them. As a man, just because you have sex with multiple women, doesn't mean they all love you. Just because you can have multiple women, doesn't mean you should because some of these women are more trouble than they're worth. Not to be rude, but some women are only looking for what they can get from you before moving on to the next person.

When you're dealing with women, always keep in mind that the type of attitude and energy you put forth is going to determine the type of energy you receive. For example, if you appear to be weak minded and allow women to come into your life to disrespect and take advantage of you, they will continue to do that. The reason many of these low-quality women are in your life is because they want to use you as a steppingstone. Although some of you guys may disagree with me when I say this, but I believe it takes a long time to get to know a woman. It's vital to evaluate a woman's character before committing to a serious relationship.

In this current society that we're in, many people are getting into relationships for the wrong reasons. Sometimes people get together because they are desperate, lonely, unstable, or broke (no money). Sadly, many people don't know how to love. In order to be in a healthy

relationship, it requires that both people show love, respect, loyalty, faithfulness, and sacrifice. If

you or your significant other can't exude these characteristics that I just mentioned, then the

relationship will not be successful.

Chapter 8

Stop Taking Women Too Seriously

The problem with a lot of men in this society is that they take women too seriously, especially on an emotional level. If I'm being honest, most women are going to gravitate towards a man with power and who can provide them with stability and an emotional connection. No need to overthink this concept, because that's what most of them want. The more you stop taking women too seriously, the clearer your mind becomes.

It's also important that you stop expecting respect, loyalty, and faithfulness from some of these toxic women. Why? Well, because it's not natural for a toxic woman to be respectful, loyal, and faithful. Women who are not considered wife material often have ulterior motives for dating certain men.

A major reason you should not take non-wife material woman seriously is because most of them will try to provoke jealousy. Believe it or not, most women will tell you if they're wife material or non-wife material if you pay close attention. That's why it's important to have foresight and discernment.

Another reason you shouldn't take most women too seriously is because many of them are childish and like to play games. After receiving what she needs from a man, a low-quality woman will move on and prey on someone else. Another significant reason you shouldn't take certain women too seriously is because most of them will try to distract you from your goals. Blaming a woman for distracting you from your aspirations is not justifiable if you allowed it to happen. Therefore, the onus is on you as the man to hold yourself to a higher standard, especially when making major decisions in your life.

Advice

       As a man, you must be very careful when you bring your woman around your "friends". Why? Well, because there are very few people in this world that have loyalty and integrity. To avoid any chaos or confusion, you shouldn't be interested in bringing your woman around your friends all the time. If I'm being honest, a wife material woman shouldn't be interested in wanting to be around your friends all the time. If your woman is overly interested in being around men and hanging out with your friends, then that means she doesn't know her role as a woman. As it pertains to your friends, you might need to re-evaluate them. Keep in mind that your woman may try to entice one of your "friends" to make advances on her. When a man makes advances on his friend's significant other, it's usually out of spite and jealousy. Always remember that envy is an evil trait to have.

Thoughts: _____

_____

_____

_____

_____

_____

_____

_____

_____

_____

Chapter 9

Signs of A Toxic Relationship

Gentlemen, it's important that you all understand that if you don't know how to speak or treat your woman properly, your woman is not going to know how to speak or treat you properly. Therefore, your situation will lead to arguments, fights, domestic disputes and other unnecessary things. Trust me, it's not worth it.

I encourage you guys to not go back and forth with women. Why? Well, because many of these women are trying to find a reason to go back and forth with you. In other words, many non-wife material women thrive on negative energy and will find any excuse to be combative towards men.

If the woman you're dealing with is not willing or not mature enough to have an adult conversation with you, then it might be time to part ways. Don't hesitate to end the relationship and walk away from her. There is no need to be with a woman if she's always trying to fight with you. A wife material woman will already know how to conduct herself.

Chapter 10

Avoid The Headaches

If you decide to have more than one woman, that's fine, but always keep in mind that dealing with multiple women can lead to multiple headaches. Despite your honesty and transparency, some women may choose to forget what you tell them in order to claim victimhood and accuse you of lying. As a result, it can lead you into some serious trouble with them.

Always be careful when you're dealing with a woman, especially multiple women. If you're a guy that loves to be with more than one woman, you have to be prepared to deal with the consequences that come with that. One minute, the women act like they're okay with you having multiple women, and the next minute they're not okay with it. It's up to you as a man to determine if it's worth the trouble.

Another situation that can cause you a lot of headaches is when you decide to allow outside parties into your relationship. Sometimes involving your friends and family members in every aspect of your relationship can make matters worse. If things are going well between you and your woman, try your best to keep other people out of that dynamic. Why? Well, because misery loves company, and if a certain individual is not happy with their own life, they'll try to sabotage yours.

Chapter 11

There Are Exceptions to The Rule

Although there are many women that are not wife material, always remember that sometimes in life there are exceptions to the rule. If you're with a woman that loves and cares about you, be thankful and satisfied. If your woman is not making your life harder, consider that a blessing. As a man, all you need to do is spend more time and focus on the people in your life that care about you.

You can't spend most of your time focusing on what these non-wife material women are doing. Why? Well, because most of them are mentally ill, and psychologically disturbed. All they care about is what they can get out of you.

Are relationships difficult? Yes, they can be, but relationships are simple as well. For a relationship to thrive, it requires love, respect, faithfulness, loyalty, communication, and sacrifice. When it comes to non-wife material women, some of them don't have the capabilities to love or sacrifice for you because they're not loyal or faithful. If you come across a woman that is not faithful, that's okay because not every woman has a good heart. As a man, there is no need to have any anger, bitterness, or resentment towards any woman. Your number one priority as a man is to always maintain a level of peace within your spirit. It's crucial to recognize the various types of women out there to avoid unnecessary drama.

Chapter 12

What Is Her Role?

When you read **1Timiothy 5:14**, you'll develop a better understanding of the woman's role on this earth. Sadly, in this society that we're living in, women are taught and conditioned to believe that being a wife and having children is beneath them. Instead of being a helpmeet to men, women are encouraged to compete with them. More women are conforming to societal ideologies and becoming emotionally detached as a result of the men's inability to get their lives in order. Therefore, both men and women are now angry, lonely, bitter, and depressed.

When a woman is choosing to partake in self-destructive behavior, she's out of order. In other words, she is not fulfilling her purpose here on the earth. However, it's not always the woman's fault. In fact, most of it is our fault as men because we failed to exhibit foresight, wisdom, prudence, discernment, and compassion. When a man doesn't exhibit these characteristics, it makes it harder for the woman to understand her role.

Many women may not want to hear this, but a large part of the woman's validation of her existence is going to come from a strong, astute, and upstanding man. Please understand that a woman seeking validation from her man is not necessarily a bad thing, especially if he's a high caliber man. Why? Well, because nothing makes a man feel better than a virtuous woman. It's important to understand that the most high God created the woman so she can be a gift for the man. With that being said, it's the man's responsibility to not take that gift for granted. That's why it's important for the man to love, honor, and cherish the woman.

Chapter 13

Don't Have Poor Taste

It is apparent that a major reason many of you guys are having issues with women is because many of you have a poor taste in them, especially when it comes to picking a wife. A man's poor choice in women reflects his self-image. A man's poor selection of women may indicate a lack of proper guidance, training, or coaching from his father.

However you decide to assess this, the man must be careful of the type of woman he impregnates. The ability to recognize a wife material woman from a non-wife material woman is important for men to know, as they can pass on this knowledge to their sons. Sharing this information with your son and other young men is of utmost importance. Most men don't know the type of situation they're getting themselves into when they engage in a rapport with women.

As a man, don't get caught up in unproductive and circular conversations with women. Going back and forth with random low-quality women is not a wise choice because it leads nowhere. However, if you are going back and forth with a woman, hopefully she's a family member of yours or she's a woman that you're currently intimate with. Stop engaging with the woman if she is not contributing anything valuable to your life.

Men need to realize that women are often overly obsessed with platonic interactions with them. To resolve this issue, men must establish boundaries and higher standards. When it comes to communicating and interacting with women, men must also establish the rules of engagement. In order to have a better chance at a healthy rapport with women, you must respect and value yourself as a man. Along with that, it's important to learn how to radiate positive energy when you're around women. Believe it or not, being astute and upstanding as a man will make a

woman respect and value you as a blessing in her company.

Chapter 14

Knowing The Difference

Gentlemen, as I mentioned earlier, just because you can have multiple women, it doesn't mean you should. It is extremely important for men to understand the difference between a wife material woman and a non-wife material woman. Why? Well, because understanding the difference between the two is going to determine certain outcomes for your life.

Sadly, most men do not know how to differentiate between a wife material woman and a non-wife material woman. Many of the women you encounter in this society are going to be low-quality women. Because most men don't know what a high-quality woman looks like, they end up putting the low-quality woman on a pedestal. That's why it's important for men to increase their level of knowledge and wisdom, especially from a spiritual standpoint. It's imperative for men to understand that a lot of women in this society are an open vessel for demons. Women's erratic behavior is often attributed to their search for spiritual sustenance. Therefore, men must take on the responsibility of teaching and guiding their women on a spiritual level.

Prior to meeting up with a woman, it's imperative for you as the man to figure out if the woman should be taken seriously. Most low-quality women spend most of their time self destructing and seeking unnecessary attention. Gentlemen, please don't put yourself on an emotional roller coaster ride with these women. Your weakness towards women could lead you to the courts, the hospital, prison, or even the graveyard if you're not careful. Always remember that the job of a wife is to make things easier for you, not harder. As she brings happiness into your life, your duty is to become the best version of yourself, elevate your level of existence and please the most high God. As a man, you should also make sure you're doing everything you can to not bring any form of instability or negativity into the woman's life.

No disrespect, but a low-quality woman should never be taken seriously, especially if she's making your life harder. Please understand that a wife is someone who will always be concerned with your health, happiness, and peace of mind. Now keep in mind that it's going to take a long time for you to determine how sincere the woman will be towards you. Why is it going to take a long time? Well, because most women are skilled at lying, cheating, and pretending. Sometimes the more valuable a man is, the longer the woman may hide her true self, especially if she knows he has a lot to offer.

Gentlemen, if you ever run into a good woman, make sure you treat her well and love her appropriately. In other words, don't become obsessed or overly infatuated with her because that can lead to you doing unhealthy and regretful things. Although women are beautiful, her true beauty comes from within. Most low-quality women rely on their appearance to deceive and manipulate men, and sadly, many men fall for it.

Does the woman you're with treat you well? How does she handle adversity? Does she understand reciprocity? How are you treating her? If you have a good woman, treat her like a good woman. If you're dealing with a non-wife material woman, it's okay to part ways and end the relationship. Not saying you have to be paranoid, but when you're interacting with certain people in your life, you must know why you're with them.

Chapter 15

Understanding The Repercussions

In this society, there are people who feel like they're entitled to do whatever they want without dealing with the repercussions. Gentlemen, it's important that you all understand that there are consequences for the things we do and don't do. As it pertains to non-wife material women, many of them have a sense of entitlement. Putting these types of women on a pedestal is a detriment to your health and well-being.

Getting to know a woman thoroughly takes a long time, as I mentioned earlier. Now, are you going to have issues with your woman/women from time to time? Yes, you are, because that's part of the relationship. If the relationship becomes toxic and you notice how wicked and inordinately angry the woman gets, then it's time to leave the relationship.

One of the major things a man should never do is allow the woman to establish the rules of engagement in the relationship. To protect your sanity, never let the woman dictate everything in the relationship. If you're not careful, some of these women will start viewing you as their subordinate. When they view you as a subordinate, they believe they have authority over you. Once they believe they have authority over you, they lose respect for you. Once they lose respect for you, they will emasculate you. Most men in this society are accustomed to being emasculated by women. They were taught at a young age that being emasculated is a normal part of a relationship, even though it's not. To make sure this doesn't happen, you must set the tone as the man from the very beginning by being consistent with your rules and standards. Please keep in mind that if the woman does not want to abide by your rules and standards, leave the relationship and tell her and move on the something else.

One of the worst mistakes a man can make in this society is to impregnate or get married to a toxic woman. That's why it's important for you as a man to know exactly what you want from these women and what you want from yourself. Be meticulous in your interactions with women. Having a better understanding of women will enable you to distinguish between a wife material woman and a non-wife material woman.

Most of the issues men face (especially black men) is based on their lack of understanding between a wife material woman and a non-wife material woman. Why? Well, it's because the man hasn't risen to the level of kingship. When he reaches that level, he can differentiate between a woman suitable for marriage and a woman who isn't.

It is apparent there is so much friction between men and women. Why are most women in this society not being raised to embrace their role as a wife and a mother? It's because most men (black men) don't view themselves as husbands and fathers. Sadly, most men only view themselves as just a sperm donor. Why? Well, it's because too many men grow up without fathers. To better our circumstances as men, we must break the cycle and change the paradigm.

Notes

END

www.ingramcontent.com/pod-product-compliance
Lightning Source LLC
Chambersburg PA
CBHW081529040426
42447CB00013B/3389